OPEN SESAME
English as a Second Language Series

PRAIRIE DAWN'S
PURPLE BOOK

Children's Television Workshop

Author

Jane Zion Brauer

Illustrators

Ellen Appleby

Tom Brannon

Mary Grace Eubank

Maggie Swanson

Photographer

Simon Baigelman

Oxford University Press

Oxford University Press

200 Madison Avenue
New York, NY 10016 USA

Walton Street
Oxford OX2 6DP England

OXFORD is a trademark of Oxford
University Press.

Library of Congress Cataloging in
Publication Data

Zion, Jane S.
  Prairie Dawn's purple book.

  (Open Sesame)
  Summary: This fourth in a series of
six includes a student book, teacher's
book, activity book, and duplicating
masters for teaching English as a second
language to ages five to ten. Focuses on
the four skills: listening, speaking, reading, and writing, using songs, stories,
conversations, games, etc.
  1. English language—Textbooks for
foreign speakers—Juvenile literature.
[1. English language—Textbooks for foreign speakers] I. Children's Television
Workshop. II. Title. III. Series.
PE 1128.Z55 1985 428.2′4 84-20753
ISBN 0-19-434161-5

The publisher would like to thank the
following for their participation in the
photography sessions:
Students and teachers of P.S. 282 at 180
6th Avenue, Brooklyn, New York; Brooklyn Children's Museum, the world's first
museum for children; Thomas Hewitt,
sculptor of papier maché dinosaurs.

The publisher would like to thank the
following for permission to reproduce
photographs: Junebug Clark, Photo Researchers; Roger A. Clark, Jr., Photo Researchers; New York Convention &
Visitors Bureau; New York State Department of Commerce; Porterfield-Chicker-
ing, Photo Researchers; Ray Woolfe,
Photo Researchers.

The publisher would like to thank Tom
Cooke for permission to reproduce the
Sesame Street characters on the inside
front and back covers.

Developmental Editor: Debbie Sistino

Printing (last digit): 9 8

Printed in Hong Kong

PREFACE

Prairie Dawn's Purple Book is for children learning English as a Second Language who already have some proficiency in listening, speaking, reading, and writing. Students improve and expand upon these skills while developing their knowledge of history, geography, science, and math. Each of the lessons follows a carefully sequenced curriculum from topic to function to structure. Topics relate to subjects children are studying in their other classes. The functions and structures reviewed and introduced are ones that help children understand and convey information on the particular topics.

The focus is on all four skills. Children will develop their language abilities through songs, chants, conversations, poems, stories, and games all based on illustrations and photographs in the book. By the end of the *Purple Book*, children are reading stories, writing reports, and holding conversations.

Other components at this level include a Teacher's Book, an Activity Book, and Cassettes.

CONTENTS

UNIT 1

Meet Jennifer Lane. She is a new neighbor on Sesame Street. She lives at 456 Sesame Street. Her telephone number is 562-9045. She is ten years old. She lives with her mother, father, grandmother, and brother, Joey. Joey is seven years old. Jennifer and Joey like to play hide and seek with their new friends on Sesame Street. Turn the page and try to find their friends!

1

Find Jennifer's New Friends

1, 2, 3, 4, 5, 6, 7, 8, 9, 10, 11, 12, 13, 14, 15, 16, 17, 18, 19, 20.
Ready or not, here I come!

Where is everybody?

3

- What do you like to do after school?
- I like to paint pictures.

- What does he like to do after school?
- He likes to paint pictures.

4

paint pictures

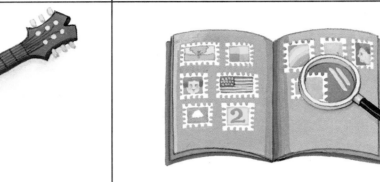

write letters

play the guitar

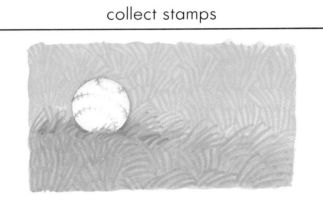

collect stamps

watch TV

play ball

bake cookies

read books

6

SHARE IT

Tell me about yourself.

1. What's your name?
2. What's your age?
3. What's your address?
4. What's your telephone number?
5. What are your hobbies?

1. Peter lives near Sesame Street. He lives with his mother, father, grandmother, grandfather, four sisters, and three brothers. How many people live in Peter's house?

2. Bert likes to collect paper clips. He has 35 paper clips. He wants to have 49 paper clips. How many more paper clips does Bert need?

3. It's 3:00. Jennifer wants to play with Prairie Dawn. First she has to deliver her newspapers for one half-hour. When can she play with Prairie Dawn?

4. It's 4:30. Jennifer is playing at Grover's house. She has to go home for dinner in one half-hour. What time does she have to go home?

I. LISTENING TEST   Pick A, B, or C.

1. (A)   (B)   (C)

2. (A)   (B)   (C)

3. (A)   (B)   (C)

4. (A)   (B)   (C)

II. READING TEST   Pick A, B, or C.

Prairie Dawn __(5)__ baby-sit for the Smiths after school. __(6)__ house
is near Sesame Street. The __(7)__ is 125 Main Street. Prairie Dawn
is going to call the Smiths before she leaves her house. Their
__(8)__ is 679-7300.

5. (A) has   (B) has to   (C) have
6. (A) They   (B) There   (C) Their
7. (A) address   (B) telephone number   (C) street
8. (A) address   (B) telephone number   (C) age

9

UNIT 2

1. It's the first day of school for Jennifer and her brother. Jennifer doesn't know how to get to school. She calls Bert.

2. Jennifer's mother gives her a package to mail. She doesn't know how to get to the post office. She calls Bert.

    Can you tell Jennifer how to go:
    - from school to 456 Sesame Street?
    - from the shoe store to the drugstore?
    - from her apartment to the hospital?

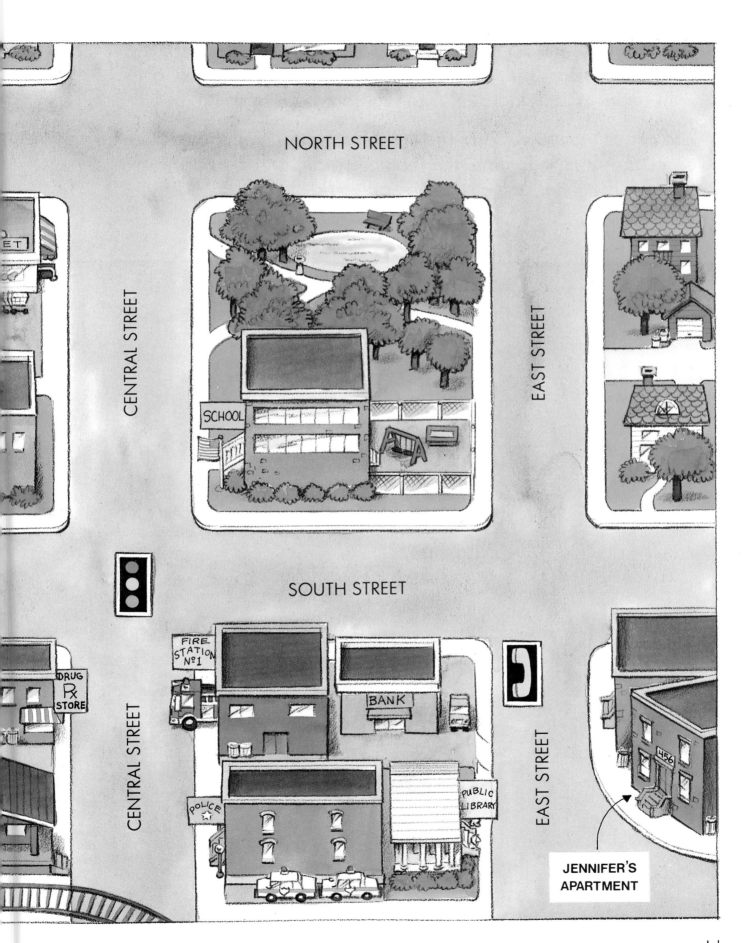

This is a map of the earth. There are seven continents. They are Africa, Antarctica, Asia, Australia, Europe, South America, and North America. The continents are big bodies of land.

There are five oceans. They are the Antarctic Ocean, the Arctic Ocean, the Atlantic Ocean, the Indian Ocean, and the Pacific Ocean. The oceans are big bodies of water.

Arctic Ocean

Pacific Ocean

The equator is an imaginary line. It goes around the middle of the earth. Everything above the equator is in the north. Everything below the equator is in the south.

Where are you from? Find it on the map!

North America
South America
Antarctica
Europe
Africa
Australia
Asia
ocean

N
W   E
S

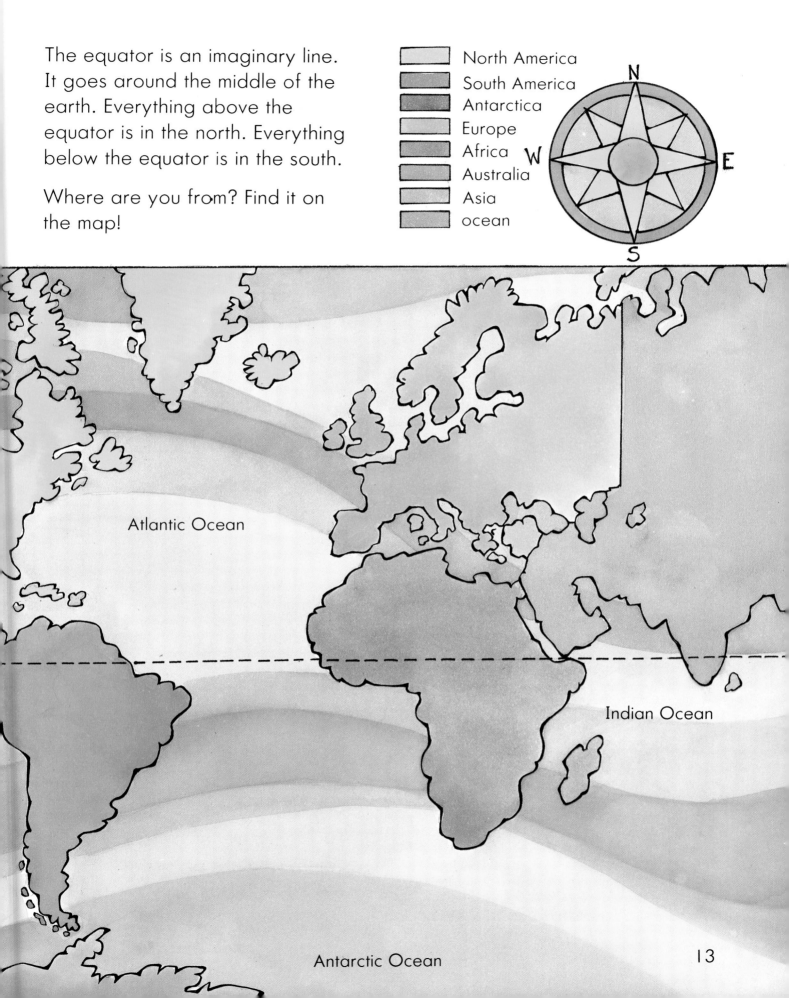

Atlantic Ocean

Indian Ocean

Antarctic Ocean

13

North, South, East, West

You can travel anywhere
North, south, east, or west.
Anywhere, it's up to you—
Go where you like best.

See new things along the way.
See them all around.
Mountains high and rivers deep—
Beauty, up and down.

Oceans blue and forests green,
Deserts with pink sand.
Quiet towns and noisy cities,
Sounds of sea and land.

You can travel anywhere
North, south, east, or west.
Anywhere, it's up to you—
Go where you like best.

SHARE IT

How do I get to your house?

Helpful Words

Turn left.
Turn right.
Go straight.
block
stoplight
corner

1. Bert went to a pigeon convention in Birdville. It was far away. It took him three days to get there. The first day he traveled 378 kilometers. The second day he traveled 259 kilometers, and the third day he traveled 197 kilometers. How many kilometers did he travel in all?

2. Rodeo Rosie went to a rodeo in Rope-'em Ridge. It was far away. It took her three days to get there. She drove for seven hours each day. How many hours did she drive in all?

3. Big Bird is going bird-watching on Peek's Peak. He has to travel 721 kilometers to get there. Today he traveled 389 kilometers. How many more kilometers does he have to travel?

4. Grover Knover is going to the circus in Clowntown. It's 96 kilometers from Sesame Street. He traveled 89 kilometers and stopped at a gas station for directions. How many more kilometers does he have to travel?

I. LISTENING TEST   Pick A, B, or C.

○ = stop sign |8| = traffic light |℃| = phone booth

1. Ⓐ at the train station   Ⓑ at the hospital   Ⓒ at the post office
2. Ⓐ at the police station   Ⓑ at the park   Ⓒ at the gas station
3. Ⓐ at the drugstore   Ⓑ at the hospital   Ⓒ at the restaurant
4. Ⓐ at the post office   Ⓑ at the school   Ⓒ at the train station

II. READING TEST   Pick A, B, or C.

5. There are _____ continents on the earth.
   Ⓐ five   Ⓑ six   Ⓒ seven
6. There are _____ oceans on the earth.
   Ⓐ five   Ⓑ six   Ⓒ seven
7. Asia is _____.
   Ⓐ an ocean   Ⓑ a continent Ⓒ a country
8. The imaginary line that goes around the earth is called the _____.
   Ⓐ equator   Ⓑ continent   Ⓒ ocean

UNIT 3

The Plant Poem

A plant needs  and
To make food to survive.

A plant has ✳ in the soil,
Drinking water to stay alive.

The 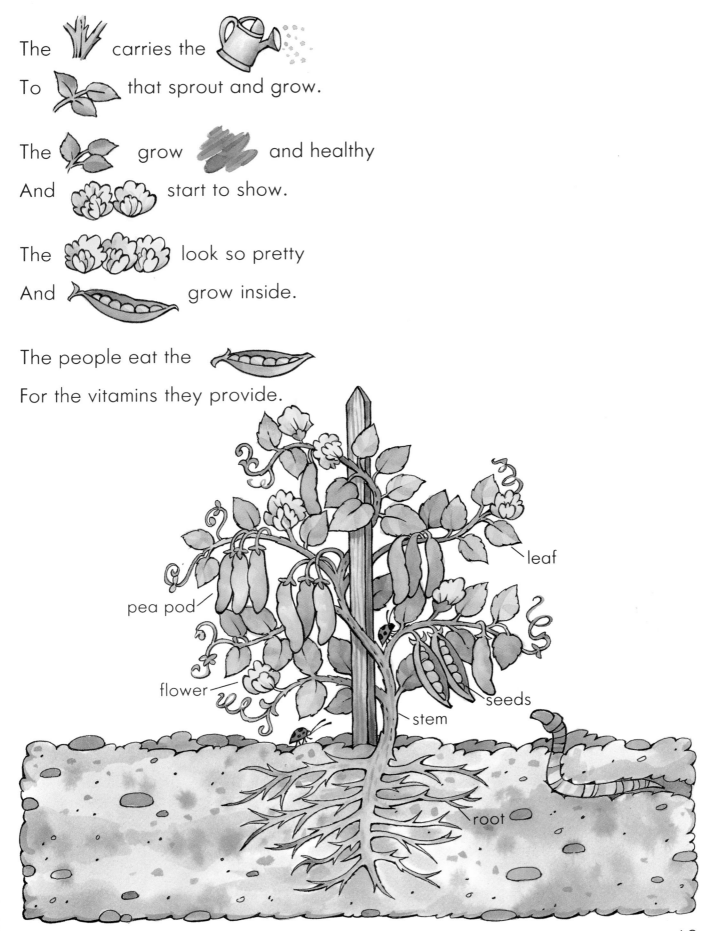 carries the 🪣 💧
To 🌿 that sprout and grow.

The 🌿 grow ☁️ and healthy
And 🥬🥬 start to show.

The 🥬🥬🥬 look so pretty
And 🫛 grow inside.

The people eat the 🫛
For the vitamins they provide.

pea pod

flower

leaf

seeds

stem

root

19

An Imaginary Plant

Cookie Monster loves to eat fruits and vegetables. Fruits and vegetables come from different parts of plants. Cookie Monster loves to eat carrots and sweet potatoes. They are the roots of plants. He loves to eat celery and asparagus. They are the stems of plants. He loves to eat lettuce and spinach. They are the leaves of plants. He loves to eat tomatoes and apples. They are the fruits of plants. He loves to eat corn and peas. They are the seeds of plants. Cookie Monster loves to eat fruits and vegetables. Mmmm! Mmmm, good!

PRAIRIE DAWN: How much are the green peppers?

MR. MACINTOSH: They're 39¢ a pound.

PRAIRIE DAWN: O.K. I'll take two pounds of green peppers.

MR. MACINTOSH: Will that be all?

PRAIRIE DAWN: Yes.

MR. MACINTOSH: That will be 78¢.

PRAIRIE DAWN: Here you are.

MR. MACINTOSH: Thank you.

BEETS
43¢/lb.

PEAS
27¢/lb.

GREEN
PEPPERS
39¢/lb.

SWEET
POTATOES
23¢/lb.

PUMPKINS
17¢/lb.

CORN
$1.03/dz.

SPECIALS
TODAY

EGGPLANT
21¢/lb.

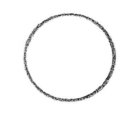

SHARE IT

- Guess what I have for you to eat!
  It may be a stem or it may be a leaf.
  Guess what I have for you to eat!
- Is it round?
- No, it's not.
- Is it long?
- Yes, it is!
- Is it green?

- No, it's not.
- Is it orange?
- Yes, it is.
- Is it a stem?
- No, it's not.
- Is it a root?
- Yes, it is.
- Is it a carrot?
- Yes! It is! It's a carrot! Here!

1. Cookie Monster needs some vegetables. He goes to Mr. MacIntosh's vegetable stand. He has $15.00. He spends $13.74. How much money does he have left?

2. Betty Lou buys three pounds of potatoes. How much does she spend?

3. Bert buys two heads of broccoli. How much does he spend?

4. The Countess buys three pounds of spinach. How much does she spend?

5. The Count buys a head of cauliflower, a pound of potatoes, a head of broccoli, and a pound of mushrooms. How much does he spend?

I. LISTENING TEST   Pick A, B, or C.

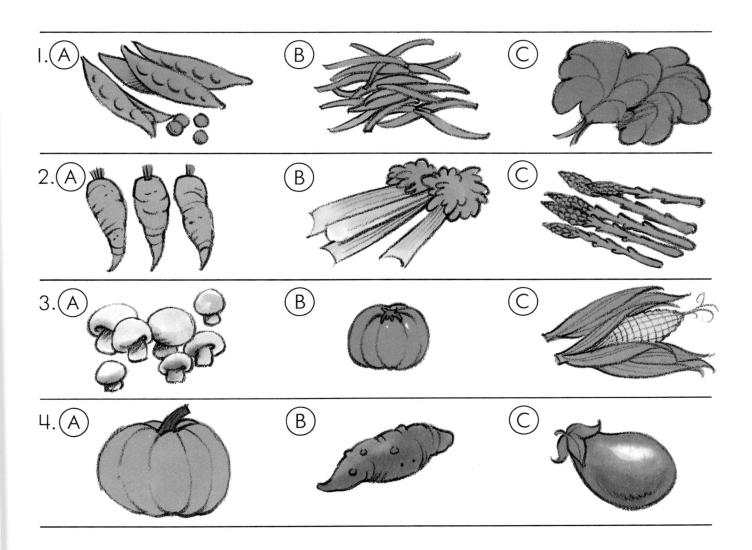

1. (A)   (B)   (C)

2. (A)   (B)   (C)

3. (A)   (B)   (C)

4. (A)   (B)   (C)

II. READING TEST   Pick A, B, C, or D.

(A) celery   (B) cauliflower   (C) spinach   (D) pea

5. Point to a leaf.   (A) (B) (C) (D)
6. Point to a stem.   (A) (B) (C) (D)
7. Point to a seed.   (A) (B) (C) (D)
8. Point to a flower.   (A) (B) (C) (D)

UNIT 4

The forest is cool, dark, and wet. The plants have thin leaves. Tall trees provide shade. Ferns grow along the ground.

Many animals live in the forest. Some of them live in the trees. Some live on the ground. Others make their homes under the ground. Can you find them?

The desert is hot and dry. It does not rain very often. The plants and animals that live in the desert need to save water. The plants have thick skin and round, thick leaves. The leaves hold a lot of water. The animals also have thick skin. This protects them from the hot sun. They drink a lot of water at one time.

The ocean is very deep. The water is salty. Plants called algae grow in the ocean. Algae have no roots, no leaves, no flowers, and no seeds. Many fish, shellfish, and mammals live in the ocean. Some are very small and some are very large.

The jungle is very hot and wet. Sometimes it is called a rain forest. Jungles are near the equator. Thousands of plants, animals, and insects live very close together. There are different layers of life in the jungle. It is dark and damp on the ground. It gets lighter and drier as you move toward the sky.

PRAIRIE DAWN: Hello, this is Prairie Dawn reporting live from the jungle. Today we're going to talk with Charlie the Chimpanzee. Hi, Charlie! How are you today?

CHARLIE: Just fine, thank you.

PRAIRIE DAWN: I hear that you lived in many places before you came to the jungle.

CHARLIE: That's right!

PRAIRIE DAWN: Where were you born?

CHARLIE: I was born in the zoo.

PRAIRIE DAWN: I see. Were you happy in the zoo?

CHARLIE: No, I wasn't. I escaped from the zoo. I wanted to be free.

PRAIRIE DAWN: Where did you go first?

CHARLIE: I went to the desert.

PRAIRIE DAWN: Were you happy there?

CHARLIE: No, I wasn't. It wasn't right for me. It was too dry and I was very thirsty. There weren't any chimps living there, so I left.

30

PRAIRIE DAWN: Where did you go next?

CHARLIE: I went to the forest.

PRAIRIE DAWN: Were you happy there?

CHARLIE: No, I wasn't. It wasn't right for me. It was too cold and there weren't any chimps living there, so I left.

PRAIRIE DAWN: Where did you go after that?

CHARLIE: I went to the ocean.

PRAIRIE DAWN: Were you happy there?

CHARLIE: No, I wasn't. It wasn't right for me. I can't swim or breathe like a fish. There weren't any chimps living there, so I left.

PRAIRIE DAWN: Where did you finally go?

CHARLIE: I came here to the jungle. There are lots of trees to swing on, lots of chimps to play with, and lots of bananas for me to eat. I love the jungle.

PRAIRIE DAWN: Thank you, Charlie. This is Prairie Dawn, signing off. Good-bye from the jungle.

31

SHARE IT

Any place where plants and animals live is a *habitat.* The forest, desert, ocean, and jungle are all habitats. Each habitat is different.

I'll ask the questions. From the answers you give,
I'll guess who you are and then where you live!

1. Are you a plant or an animal?
2. What do you look like?
3. What do you like to eat?
4. Is your habitat hot or cold, wet or dry, sunny or dark?

I. LISTENING TEST   Pick A, B, or C.

1. Ⓐ   Ⓑ   Ⓒ

2. Ⓐ   Ⓑ   Ⓒ

3. Ⓐ   Ⓑ   Ⓒ

4. Ⓐ   Ⓑ   Ⓒ

II. READING TEST   Pick A, B, C, or D.

Ⓐ rabbit   Ⓑ camel   Ⓒ parrot   Ⓓ crab

These animals all live in different habitats. Read the questions and point to the correct animals.

5. Who lives in the desert?   Ⓐ Ⓑ Ⓒ Ⓓ
6. Who lives in the jungle?   Ⓐ Ⓑ Ⓒ Ⓓ
7. Who lives in the forest?   Ⓐ Ⓑ Ⓒ Ⓓ
8. Who lives in the ocean?   Ⓐ Ⓑ Ⓒ Ⓓ

UNIT 5

Building Barkley's Doghouse

One day, Big Bird was walking down Sesame Street. He saw Betty Lou sitting by herself next to a pile of wood.

"Hi, Betty Lou. What are you doing?" asked Big Bird.

"It's Barkley's birthday. I want to build him a doghouse, but I can't do it by myself," answered Betty Lou. "I have some wood, but I need a saw to cut it."

"I'll help you find a saw," said Big Bird.

Big Bird and Betty Lou continued down Sesame Street. They saw Grover sitting by himself holding a saw.

"Hi, Grover. What are you doing?" asked Big Bird.

"I want to build a doghouse for Barkley, but I can't do it by myself," answered Grover. "I have a saw, but I need wood, a hammer, and nails."

"We have some wood," said Betty Lou.

"We'll help you find a hammer and some nails," said Big Bird.

35

Big Bird, Betty Lou, and Grover continued down Sesame Street. They saw Bert and Ernie sitting by themselves. Ernie was holding a hammer. Bert was holding some nails.

"Hi, Ernie and Bert. What are you doing?" asked Big Bird.

"We want to build a doghouse for Barkley, but we can't do it by ourselves," they answered. "We have a hammer and nails, but we need a saw and some wood."

"Let's see," said Big Bird. "You can't build Barkley's doghouse by yourselves. Betty Lou can't build it by herself. Grover can't build it by himself. Let's build it together!"

Betty Lou, Grover, Bert, Ernie, and Big Bird shared their saw, hammer, nails, and wood. They worked together and built a big, beautiful doghouse for Barkley.

36

Everyone was happy, especially Barkley.

What did Oscar do yesterday?

He went to the Grouch Festival.

Who did he go with?

Nobody. He went by himself.

1. Rodeo Rosie
movies

2. you
bike riding

3. Bert and Ernie
roller skating

SHARE IT

Ask your friend:

1. What are three things you like to do by yourself?
2. What are three things you like to do with other people?
3. Did you ever cooperate with other people to do something special? What did you do?

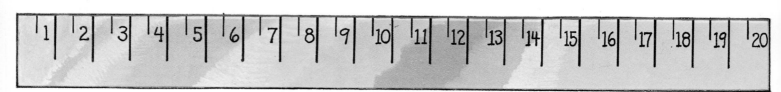

Betty Lou and her friends had to measure the pieces of wood before they built Barkley's doghouse. Turn to page 37. Use your ruler to measure:

1. the length of the left side of the roof.
2. the length of the right side of the roof.
3. the height of the left side of the doghouse.
4. the height of the right side of the doghouse.
5. the height of the door.
6. the width of the doghouse.

Which measurements are the same? Why?

Can you draw something interesting with your ruler? Try it!

I. LISTENING TEST Pick A, B, or C.

cm = centimeters

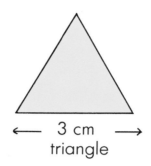
3 cm
triangle

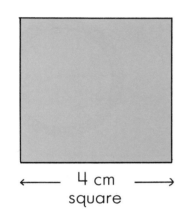
4 cm
square

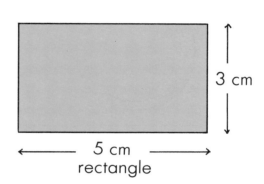
3 cm

5 cm
rectangle

(A) 3 centimeters   (B) 4 centimeters   (C) 5 centimeters

1. (A)   (B)   (C)
2. (A)   (B)   (C)
3. (A)   (B)   (C)
4. (A)   (B)   (C)

II. READING TEST Pick A, B, or C.

5. We baked the cake all by _____.
   (A) themselves   (B) myself   (C) ourselves

6. She went to the movies all by _____.
   (A) himself   (B) herself   (C) yourself

7. They built the doghouse all by _____.
   (A) themselves   (B) yourselves   (C) ourselves

8. I went bike riding all by _____.
   (A) myself   (B) yourself   (C) herself

41

UNIT 6   LISTENING TEST   Pick A, B, or C.

READING TEST   Pick A, B, or C.

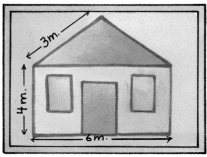

1. (A) It's 3:20. She has to deliver newspapers.
   (B) It's 3:45. She has to deliver newspapers.
   (C) It's 3:50. She has to deliver newspapers.

2. (A) The school is on the left, across the street from the hospital.
   (B) The school is on the right, across the street from the supermarket.
   (C) The school is on the right, across the street from the gas station.

3. (A) This continent is above the equator.
   (B) This continent is below the equator.
   (C) This continent is on the equator.

4. (A) This is a fern. It grows in the jungle.
   (B) This is a cactus. It grows in the desert.
   (C) This is algae. It grows in the ocean.

5. (A) The height of this house is 4 meters.
   (B) The height of this house is 6 meters.
   (C) The width of this house is 4 meters.

READING TEST   Pick A, B, or C.

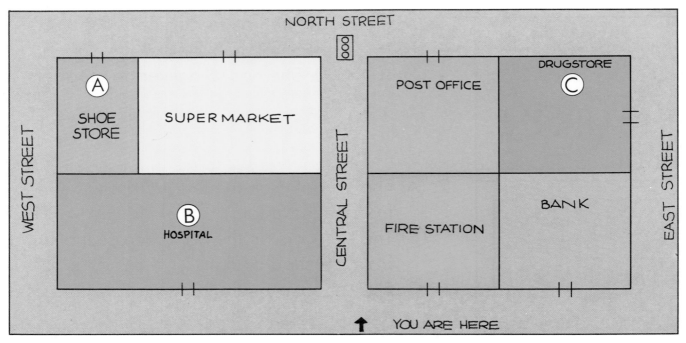

1. Walk one block up Central Street. Turn left at the traffic light.
   Walk one block down North Street. This place is on your left.
   Where are you?

2. This is an animal. It is brown. It lives in the forest,
   and it runs very fast.

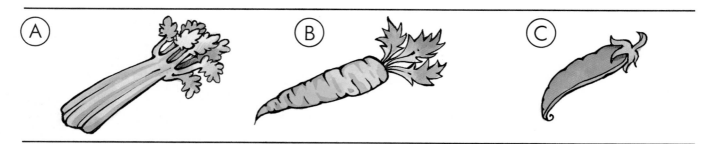

3. This is a vegetable we eat. It is long, thin, and green.
   It is the stem of the plant.

WRITING TEST

A. Charlie the Chimpanzee ran away from the zoo when he was little. First he went to the desert, but it was too dry for him. Next he went to the forest, but it was too cold for him. Then he went to the ocean, but it was too wet for him. Finally he went to the jungle. He loved the jungle. There were lots of trees to swing on, lots of bananas to eat, and lots of chimps to play with. Charlie is living happily in the jungle.

What's the answer?
1. Who ran away from the zoo?
2. Where did he go first?
3. Where did he go next?
4. What was the best habitat for Charlie?
5. Why did he like the jungle?

B. It is Wednesday afternoon. Jennifer and Joey are at home. Jennifer is baby-sitting for Joey. They are playing checkers. Jennifer likes to baby-sit for Joey because they always have fun. Their mother will be home at 5:00, and they will all eat dinner together.

What's the question?
1. Who . . . ?
2. What . . . ?
3. Where . . . ?
4. Why . . . ?
5. When . . . ?

WRITING TEST

What's the word?

A. THE GREAT IDEA

One Saturday morning, and were sitting and

thinking about what to do. Prairie Dawn had an idea.

"Let's build a for your ," she said.

"Great idea!" said Bert.

Bert got the  and the . Prairie Dawn got the

the , and the . First they measured the

Next, they cut it and nailed it together. Then they painted the

. It was really beautiful!

B. SUPER SALAD

There was a sale at Mr. MacIntosh's vegetable stand.

were 59¢ a pound,   were 74¢ a pound,   were 49¢

a pound,   was 68¢ a bunch,   was 39¢ a head,

           were 36¢ a pound, and   were 23¢ a bunch.

The Count and Countess bought many vegetables at the sale.

Then they went home and made a delicious .

46

Just For Fun!

Do the Charlie Cha-Cha!

47

UNIT 7

The Real You

Try something different,
Try something new.
Think of a job
That will be fun for you.

What are you good at?
What can you do?
Go ahead! Dream of
What you'd like to do.

Do you want to work with
People, animals, or machines?
Do you want to work
In fancy clothes or in blue jeans?

Think of all the many things
You could do.
Think of what you like.
Find out about you!

clown   computer operator   chef   veterinarian

construction worker   baseball player   photographer   astronaut

- What do you do?
- Can you tell me about your job?

BETTY LOU: Do you work outdoors?

PRAIRIE DAWN: No, I don't.

THE COUNT: Do you work indoors?

PRAIRIE DAWN: Yes, I do.

BERT: Do you wear a uniform?

PRAIRIE DAWN: No, I don't.

BETTY LOU: Do you work with animals?

PRAIRIE DAWN: No, I don't.

THE COUNT: Do you work with people?

PRAIRIE DAWN: Sometimes.

BERT: Do you work with machines?

PRAIRIE DAWN: Yes, I do.

BETTY LOU: Do you work on a computer?

PRAIRIE DAWN: Yes, I do.

THE COUNT: Are you a computer operator?

PRAIRIE DAWN: Yes, I am!

SHARE IT

Interview an adult. It may be your mother, father, aunt, uncle, grandparent, or a friend. Find out about his or her job.

1. What do you do?
2. Where do you work?
3. How many days a week do you work?
4. What are some of the things you do each day?
5. What's the best thing about your job?
6. What's the worst thing about your job?
7. Do you want to change your job some day? Why?

1. Chef Cookie Monster had $50.00. He spent $37.29 at Mr. MacIntosh's vegetable stand. How much money does he have left?

2. Barkley's paw hurts. He needs three tubes of medicine from the veterinarian. Each tube costs $9.00. How much does the medicine cost?

3. Prairie Dawn is a computer operator. Next week, she will work from 9:00 A.M. to 5:00 P.M. each day. She will go to lunch from 12:00 to 1:00. How many hours will she work each day?

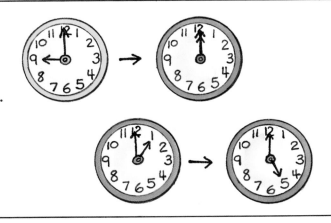

4. Bert wants to be a photographer. He will work seven hours each day. He will work five days each week. How many hours will he work each week?

A Day in the Life of Chef Cookie Monster

Chef Cookie Monster works in a restaurant. He wakes up early every day. First he goes shopping for all the food he needs. Then he brings the food to the big kitchen in the restaurant.

Chef Cookie Monster and his helpers busily prepare the food. They carefully cut, slice, and chop up the fruits and vegetables. Then they cook the fish and meat. Chef Cookie Monster bakes the desserts himself.

54

At 11:00 the restaurant opens for lunch. Waiters and waitresses quickly run into the kitchen with their orders. Chef Cookie Monster proudly cooks a perfect meal each time! And luckily, he never forgets the dessert!

I. LISTENING TEST   Pick A, B, or C.

II. READING TEST   Pick A, B, or C.

Chef Cookie Monster works at a great French restaurant. He works hard all day. Every morning, he __(5)__ shopping at the market. Then he and his helpers __(6)__ the food. Chef Cookie Monster __(7)__ the desserts by himself. When the food is ready, the waiters and waitresses __(8)__ to the kitchen to pick up their orders.

5. Ⓐ go   Ⓑ going   Ⓒ goes
6. Ⓐ prepare   Ⓑ preparing   Ⓒ prepares
7. Ⓐ bake   Ⓑ baking   Ⓒ bakes
8. Ⓐ run   Ⓑ running   Ⓒ runs

UNIT 8

My pencil is very long.
Really? My pencil is longer than your pencil!

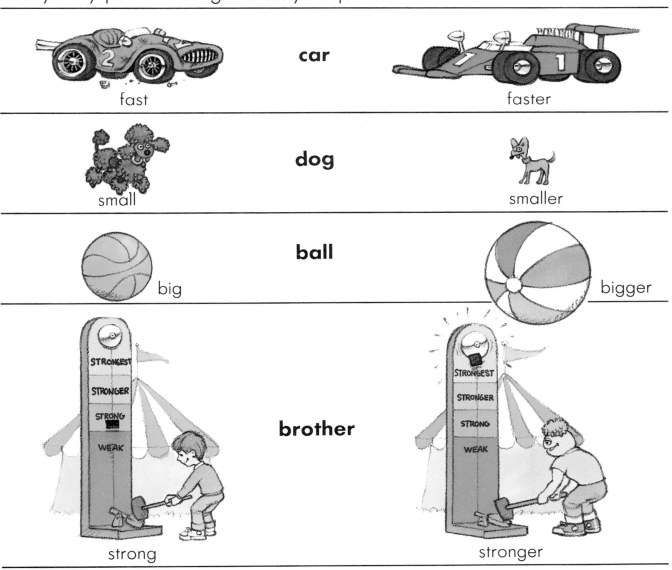

car

fast   faster

dog

small   smaller

ball

big   bigger

brother

strong   stronger

THE ADVENTURES OF PRAIRIE DAWN
Prairie Dawn's Journey

One day Prairie Dawn saw Dr. Nobel Price working on his newest project, a big machine. Prairie Dawn walked into the machine. Clang! The door slammed behind her.

"Oh, no!" shouted Dr. Price. "Prairie Dawn is trapped in my time machine!"

Prairie Dawn saw some buttons on the wall inside. She pressed one. The machine took off and she tumbled around inside. Then the machine stopped, the door opened, and Prairie Dawn fell out.

"Where am I?" she asked.

She looked around. This place looked very different from Sesame Street. There weren't any buildings, cars, or trucks. Prairie Dawn didn't see any of her friends.

"Hello, hello!" she called.

Nobody answered. Prairie Dawn felt scared. All of a sudden a huge, strange-looking animal appeared. It had a pointy head, a large, humped back, four fat legs, and a long tail. It stared at Prairie Dawn. Then it smiled, and she wasn't scared anymore.

58

Prairie Dawn was back in the time of dinosaurs. Dinosaurs were animals that lived millions and millions of years ago, when there were no people. The weather was always warm. The world looked like a big jungle. There were many kinds of dinosaurs. There were big ones, small ones, fast ones, and slow ones. Some dinosaurs were mean and some were friendly. Luckily, Prairie Dawn found a friendly one!

TO BE
CONTINUED

Dinosaurs, dinosaurs all around,
In the air and on the ground,
Dinosaurs in the water too,
Looking at me and you.

The Longest
The Longest
Diplodocus

The Biggest
The Biggest
Brontosaurus

The Fastest
Pteranodon

The Fastest

The Smallest
Compsognathus

The Smallest

The Meanest
Tyrannosaurus Rex

The Meanest

The Bravest

The Bravest
Triceratops

- Did the Diplodocus eat more food than any other dinosaur?
- No, I don't think so. I think the Brontosaurus did. In fact, the Brontosaurus was the fattest dinosaur of all!

1. Stegosaurus—fight more
   Tyrannosaurus Rex—meanest

2. Triceratops—have more horns
   Pentaceratops—ugliest

SHARE IT

Ask your friend:

1. If you could be any dinosaur, which one would you be? Why?
2. What would you look like?
3. What would you eat?
4. What would you do? Why?

Now, draw a picture of your friend as a dinosaur!

1. A Brontosaurus was very hungry. He ate 219 leaves on Monday, 195 leaves on Tuesday, and 228 leaves on Wednesday. How many leaves did he eat altogether?

2. There were three Pentaceratopses standing together. Each one had five horns. How many horns were there in all?

3. There were 742 leaves on the tree. The Diplodocus ate 578 of them. How many leaves were left?

4. Prairie Dawn stayed in the time of dinosaurs for three days. She saw eight dinosaurs each day. How many dinosaurs did she see in all?

I. LISTENING TEST   Pick A, B, or C.

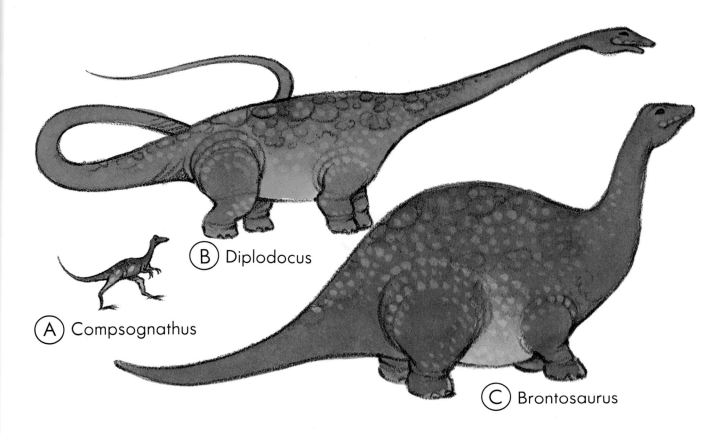

(A) Compsognathus

(B) Diplodocus

(C) Brontosaurus

1. (A)   (B)   (C)

2. (A)   (B)   (C)

3. (A)   (B)   (C)

4. (A)   (B)   (C)

II. READING TEST   Pick A, B, or C.

5. The Tyrannosaurus was _____ dinosaur.
   (A) mean   (B) the meanest   (C) meanest

6. Some dinosaurs were very _____.
   (A) brave   (B) braver   (C) bravest

7. The Brontosaurus was _____ than the Tyrannosaurus.
   (A) big   (B) bigger   (C) more

8. The Brontosaurus ate _____ food than the Diplodocus.
   (A) most   (B) much   (C) more

UNIT 9

THE ADVENTURES OF PRAIRIE DAWN
A Long Time Ago

Three days later, Prairie Dawn said good-bye to the dinosaurs. She walked into the time machine and pressed another button on the wall. The machine took off again and she tumbled around inside.

When Prairie Dawn landed, she still wasn't on Sesame Street. There weren't any dinosaurs. There were people. They didn't dress like her friends on Sesame Street. They wore clothing made from the skins of animals. Their houses didn't look like the houses on Sesame Street. They lived in grass huts.

Prairie Dawn was in a prehistoric village. The people greeted her and showed her around the village.

The people were friendly. They showed Prairie Dawn how they
made fires by rubbing sticks together. They explained how they
used fire to keep warm and to cook food. Fire was very important
to them. They also showed her how they hunted for fish in the river
and for animals in the forest. They hunted with spears.

The village was a nice place, but Prairie Dawn missed
her friends on Sesame Street. She wanted to go home.
She pressed another button in the time machine and
blasted off again.

TO BE
CONTINUED

THE ADVENTURES OF PRAIRIE DAWN
Out West

When Prairie Dawn's time machine landed again, she tumbled out the door to see a small town. There was a bank like the one on Sesame Street and a store like Mr. Hooper's store back home.

Many people were riding into town, but they didn't ride in cars or buses. Some of them rode there in stagecoaches and on horses. Others traveled slowly down the bumpy road in covered wagons.

Prairie Dawn walked around the town and met a lot of people. The blacksmith made shoes for all the horses. The owner of the general store sold food to eat and cloth to make clothes. There was a sheriff, a doctor, a lawyer, and even a broom maker.

There were many things to do in town. People took out money at the bank, ate at the restaurant, and shopped at the general store. The children went to school there.

Prairie Dawn was in a town in the Old West. In many ways it was like home, but Prairie Dawn missed her friends on Sesame Street. She said good-bye to everyone and blasted off again.

TO BE CONTINUED

69

SHARE IT

We can learn a lot about the past by speaking to our grandparents, great-aunts, or great-uncles. Interview a grandparent.

Ask:
1. Where were you born?
2. What do you remember about your mother and father?
3. Do you have any brothers and sisters? What did you do together?
4. Did you go to school? What was it like?
5. Did you help your mother and father at home? How?
6. What was the best thing that ever happened to you?
7. What was the worst thing that ever happened to you?

1. A fisherman caught 87 fish. His friends ate 59 fish that night. How many were left?

2. A woman from a prehistoric village was drawing pictures on a stone wall. She drew four fish, four deer, and four bears. How many pictures did she draw in all?

3. Prairie Dawn went to Bert's Shoe Store. She bought three pairs of shoes. Each pair cost $6.00. How much money did she spend?

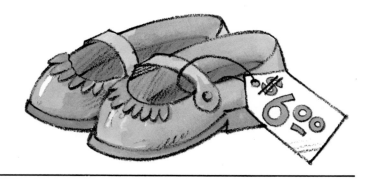

4. Bert had $7.94. He went to the supermarket. He spent $5.95. How much money does he have left?

I. LISTENING TEST   Pick the correct letter.

1. Ⓐ   Ⓑ   Ⓒ   Ⓓ   Ⓔ   Ⓕ   Ⓖ   Ⓗ
2. Ⓐ   Ⓑ   Ⓒ   Ⓓ   Ⓔ   Ⓕ   Ⓖ   Ⓗ
3. Ⓐ   Ⓑ   Ⓒ   Ⓓ   Ⓔ   Ⓕ   Ⓖ   Ⓗ
4. Ⓐ   Ⓑ   Ⓒ   Ⓓ   Ⓔ   Ⓕ   Ⓖ   Ⓗ

II. READING TEST   Pick A, B, or C.

A long time ago, fire __(5)__ very important. People __(6)__ fires to
keep warm. They also needed fire to __(7)__ their food. They
cooked it __(8)__ over the fire.

5. Ⓐ is   Ⓑ was   Ⓒ were
6. Ⓐ make   Ⓑ making   Ⓒ made
7. Ⓐ cook   Ⓑ cooks   Ⓒ cooked
8. Ⓐ slow   Ⓑ slower   Ⓒ slowly

73

UNIT 10

The Solar System

This is our solar system. It has nine planets. All the planets revolve around a star. We call this star the sun. Each planet follows its own path around the sun. We call this path an orbit.

The sun gives heat and light to all of the planets. The planet closest to the sun is Mercury. It is the hottest planet in the solar system. The planet farthest from the sun is Pluto. It is the coldest planet in the solar system. The biggest planet is Jupiter. The smallest planet is Mercury.

The planet we live on is Earth. It is between Venus and Mars. It takes 365 days for the Earth to complete one orbit, or one trip around the sun. This is how we measure a year.

Mercury	88 days
Venus	225 days
Earth	365 days
Mars	687 days
Jupiter	12 years
Saturn	30 years
Uranus	84 years
Neptune	165 years
Pluto	248 years

74

COUNT: Where's Jupiter?

COUNTESS: It's between Saturn and Mars.

COUNT: How long does it take for Jupiter to revolve
around the sun?

COUNTESS: It takes twelve years.

COUNT: Twelve wonderful years! 1, 2, 3, 4, 5, 6, 7, 8, 9,
10, 11, 12! Ha, ha, ha, ha, ha, ha!

1. It takes 365 days for the Earth to revolve around the sun once. How many days will it take for the Earth to revolve around the sun three times?

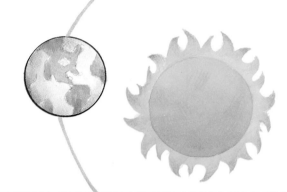

2. It takes 687 days for Mars to revolve around the sun. It takes 365 days for the Earth to revolve around the sun. How much longer does it take for Mars to revolve around the sun?

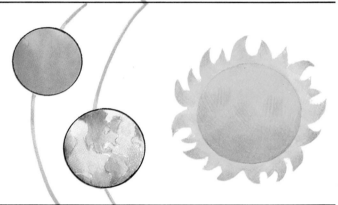

3. It takes Pluto 248 years to revolve around the sun once. How many years will it take for Pluto to revolve around the sun twice?

4. It takes Uranus 84 years to revolve around the sun. It takes Neptune 165 years to revolve around the sun. How much longer does it take for Neptune to revolve around the sun?

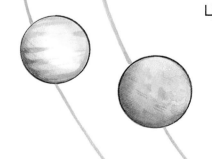

The Year 2001

Imagine the year 2001.
Think about it! It can be fun!

Imagine houses built underground,
And traveling by rocket without a sound.

Imagine a room with buttons to press
To cook your food and clean up your mess.

78

Imagine seeing friends on the telephone,
And playing with robots when you're all alone.

Imagine the year 2001.
Think about it! It can be fun!

SHARE IT

It is the year 2001. Talking about it can be lots of fun!

Ask a friend:
1. Where will you live?
2. What will your job be?
3. How will you get to work each day?
4. Where will you travel on vacation?
5. How will computers help you?
6. What will you be able to do in the year 2001 that you can't do now?

THE ADVENTURES OF PRAIRIE DAWN
Prairie Dawn Comes Home

Prairie Dawn zoomed through the sky in her time machine. When she landed, she saw many tall buildings and many people.

The people were moving quickly along the sidewalks, but they weren't walking. The sidewalks were moving! Prairie Dawn looked up in the sky and saw people in flying machines. "Beep, beep," went the heli-bus. "Honk, honk," went the heli-taxi.

Prairie Dawn climbed out of her time machine and hopped onto one of the moving sidewalks. "Hey, this is fun!" she said. She got off at a place called the Whiz Kids' School. When she walked into the office, she saw the date on a computer.

"Wow! I'm in the year 2001!" she exclaimed.

"May I help you?" asked the school secretary.

"Oh, yes, please," said Prairie Dawn. She told the secretary about her time machine and how she was trying to get home.

"You came to the right place for help," said the secretary. "Roger, please take Prairie Dawn to Miss Smith's classroom."

For the next week, everyone helped Prairie Dawn program her time machine correctly. She learned all about computers and programming.

"Roger," said Roger the Robot as he led Prairie Dawn down the hall.

Miss Smith and her class stopped their work to listen to Prairie Dawn's story. When she told them all about her adventures, they were very excited.

At the end of the week, Prairie Dawn got back into her time machine. She waved good-bye to her new friends and promised to visit them again soon.

Finally, Prairie Dawn saw a green and white sign in the distance. It said Sesame Street! Everyone at home was very happy to see her. They all hugged her and listened to her stories.

"Which place did you like best?" asked Bert.

"You know what?" said Prairie Dawn. "The place I like best of all is right here—on Sesame Street!"

THE END

I. LISTENING TEST   Pick A, B, or C.

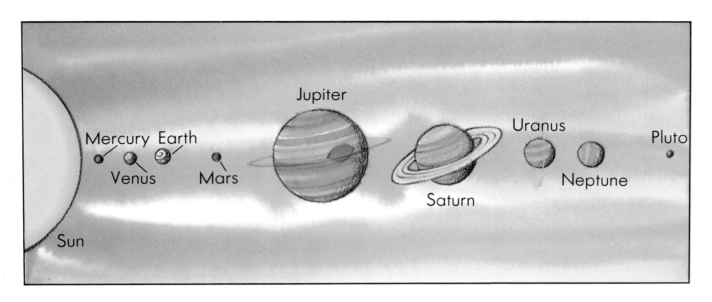

1. Ⓐ Earth   Ⓑ Jupiter   Ⓒ Neptune
2. Ⓐ Mercury   Ⓑ Venus   Ⓒ Uranus
3. Ⓐ Saturn   Ⓑ Pluto   Ⓒ Mars
4. Ⓐ Jupiter   Ⓑ Mercury   Ⓒ Saturn

II. READING TEST   Pick A, B, or C.

Prairie Dawn and her friends were sitting in a park near Sesame Street. Prairie Dawn __(5)__ her friends about her adventures.

"What __(6)__ you see?" they asked. "What __(7)__ life be like in the year 2001?"

Prairie Dawn told them all about her trip. Then she said, "I __(8)__ a wonderful time, but it's great to be home!"

5. Ⓐ will tell   Ⓑ was telling   Ⓒ were telling
6. Ⓐ do   Ⓑ did   Ⓒ will
7. Ⓐ is   Ⓑ did   Ⓒ will
8. Ⓐ have   Ⓑ having   Ⓒ had

UNIT 11

LISTENING TEST   Pick A, B, or C.

1. (A)   (B)   (C)

2. (A)   (B)   (C)

3. (A)   (B)   (C)

4. (A) BLACKSMITH   (B) HARDWARE   (C) BARBER SHOP

   Blacksmith's Shop   Hardware Store   Barbershop

5. (A)   (B)   (C)

   Pluto   Earth   Mercury

READING TEST Pick A, B, or C.

1. Ⓐ A veterinarian always works outdoors.
   Ⓑ A veterinarian helps sick animals.
   Ⓒ A veterinarian helps sick people.

2. Ⓐ The Compsognathus is the biggest dinosaur of all.
   Ⓑ The Diplodocus is longer than the Compsognathus.
   Ⓒ The Pteranodon is bigger than the Diplodocus.

3. Ⓐ This is a barber. He provides a service.
   Ⓑ This is a broom maker. He provides a service.
   Ⓒ This is a barber. He provides goods.

4. Ⓐ Earth is the biggest planet in the solar system.
   Ⓑ Jupiter is smaller than Earth.
   Ⓒ Mercury is the smallest planet in the solar system.

READING TEST   Pick A, B, or C.

Tyrannosaurus Rex   Triceratops

1. Dinosaurs lived millions and millions of years ago. This dinosaur
   was very big. It fought with the other dinosaurs. It was the
   meanest dinosaur of all.

2. In the Old West, people worked at many different jobs. This
   person wore a badge. He was like a police officer for the town.

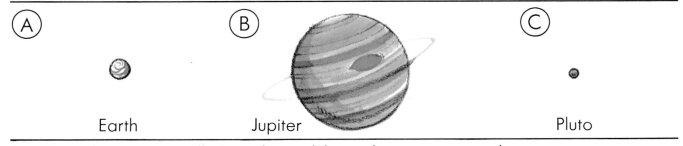

Earth   Jupiter   Pluto

3. This planet is small. It is the coldest planet in our solar system.
   It is also the farthest from the sun.

WRITING TEST

A. Ala and Dar lived in a prehistoric village. They lived in a grass hut and wore clothing made from animal skins. Fire was very important to them. They used it for cooking their food and for staying warm at night. They liked their little village.

What's the answer?
1. Who lived in a prehistoric village?
2. What kind of house did they live in?
3. What was their clothing made from?
4. When did they need to stay warm?
5. Why was fire important to them?

B. Some day I will build my own robot. Her name will be Roberta. She will live at my house. She will know how to sing, dance, and play baseball with me. Every day at five o'clock, she will clean up my toys and eat dinner with me. Then we will play wonderful computer games. We will have so much fun!

What's the question?
1. Who . . . ?
2. What . . . ?
3. Where . . . ?
4. When . . . ?
5. Why . . . ?

WRITING TEST

What's the word?

THE JOB FAIR

One day, many people came to a job fair at Big Bird's . They all did different jobs. They came to show the how they worked and to answer about their jobs.

First, Big Bird saw a doing tricks. Next, he watched a working on a . Then he saw a giving Barkley a checkup. There was a baking and an showing pictures of her spaceship to the . A was walking around taking pictures.

Big Bird enjoyed watching some build a small . There was so much to see! He wondered what kind of job he would like to have some day.

WRITING TEST

What's the word?

SATURDAY MORNING

It was Saturday morning. ___ had a list of things to buy. First she went to the ___ to buy a new pair of ___ . Then she went to the ___ to buy some ___ , ___ , and ___ . After that, she went to the department store to buy a ___ and a ___ that were on sale.

The ___ was busy, too. He had a list of things to do. He counted them: 1 , 2 , 3 , 4 . First he went to the fix-it shop to get his ___ fixed. Next, he went to the ___ to return some ___ about ___ . Then he went to the ___ to get his hair cut. The last place was the ___ . He needed gas for his Batmobile.

Prairie Dawn saw many interesting things while she was traveling.
She hid them all over page 92. Turn the page and try to find them.

92